The ABC Islands of the Caribbean

The ABC Islands of the Caribbean

A Basic Travelers Guide

Bryan Kelley

Self Published with Kindle Direct Publishing

Printed in the United States of America

First Printing, 2019

ISBN: 9781091083813

For permissions contact: curious.kelley.travel.blog@gmail.com

Cover by Bryan Kelley

Acknowledgement

My special thanks are extended to the staff of...
- Papagayo Beach Hotel
- The Dolphin Academy
- Captain Don's Habitat
- Wonders Boutique Hotel

Dedication

This book is dedicated to all couples that enjoy traveling together and that make the choice to have fun no matter what the circumstance.

"What we find in a soulmate is not something wild to tame, but something wild to run with."

— Robert Brault

Preface

When it comes to writing there is always a "*why.*" Or at least there is supposed to be.

As you may or may not know, the "*Preface*" section of a book is where the writer can let their readers in on what motivated the book to be written in the first place.

We all gain inspiration from various sources. Whether it's a mentor, a family member, or even a life-changing experience, inspiration is quite literally everywhere. The preface is where a writer can speak about whom or what inspired them to write the book.

Recently I had an experience during my travels that reminded me of how incredible travel can be. It didn't matter that everything didn't go according to plan. It didn't matter that in the middle of it all, the rug got pulled out from underneath me and everything about the trip changed because of it. The magic and the adventure were all still there for me to enjoy.

I think that most of us that have traveled can agree that traveling can improve our perspectives in life. It is safe to say that it is our ticket to our better selves if we remain open and available to how it can change us and improve us. It certainly affords us an opportunity for growth.

And this is exactly why I decided to write this book, to remind myself that I steer my own ship. There isn't a person out there that can affect me unless I allow them to. There isn't a single event that can turn my day sour unless I allow it. I travel to see new places, meet new people, eat incredible food and one of the most important reasons I travel... is to have fun.

When you read this book, that is exactly what you should keep in mind. And if you decide to travel to these incredible islands, there is plenty of fun to be had.

"The world is a book, and those who do not travel read only one page."

-Saint Augustine

Disclaimer

Welcome to my experiment!

I realize that buying and reading this book was sort of an "experiment" on your part. In a way it was a leap of faith that you might find something entertaining, enlightening, educational, or useful. And I hope that as you read through this book you will find at least some small nugget or tidbit that will be worth your while.

Please keep in mind that I am not claiming to be any sort of expert on the things that I cover in this book. I simply share my experiences with others because it contributes to my happiness, and in some ways makes it seem like my experiences might be more meaningful if they can help someone else in some way. Furthermore, when I share my experiences with everyone, I enjoy them even more than I would have if I would have kept the experiences all to myself.

Another intended goal of every book that I write is to inspire and motivate. It is my sincerest hope that anyone reading this will at some point break free of their ho hum everyday lives and get out and see the world.

One of the most important things I can tell you that I have learned about travel is that it is good for you. Whether you're traveling three states away or planning to engage in a multi-continent hop, that trip will affect a change in you. In ways that are hard to imagine, travelling will help you grow. And it will absolutely fan the flames within you to help you burn that much brighter.

As you read through this book and any book that I have written, you will see that it is very casual. I am a pretty low key fella, and I am certain that this book and my writing style will reflect that.

Enjoy!

Table of Contents

Planning Your Flight

Any vacation or trip that you plan on taking is going to start with your means of transportation. On this trip my plans began with figuring out flight dates, times etc.

As I have mentioned in other books I have written, two of the best days to fly out are typically Tuesdays and Wednesdays. What I mean by "best," is least expensive. According to a CheapAir study, if you chose these days you'll save an average of $73 per ticket. So if it is possible for you to arrange your vacation time to fly out on either of these days, you can often times save a considerable amount of money.

If you consider that one of the largest expenses on any vacation that you might have is airfare, then it makes sense to try and save any way that you can.

Take a look on the following pages at the examples I have provided. I tried to situate the illustrations sideways to take up as much of the page as possible in hopes that it would be large enough that you would actually be able to read it. However, it didn't work, so they may now be too small for some of you to read. In addition, screen shots are not of the best quality for printing. So I apologize, but these illustrations are important to show you what I am talking about so I had to work with what I had.

This screen shot was taken off of Expedia.com on 1/08/2019 which was a Tuesday and was for my departure of Tuesday 3/12/2019. I was looking for a one way flight leaving from Portland Oregon (PDX) and flying to Curacao (CUR). If you look to the left and right of the $193 that is highlighted in dark blue, you will see that most of the other days are more expensive.

** Screen shot taken on Tues Jan 8th, 2019

1

The second example that I have provided was taken off of Expedia.com on Sunday 1/13/2019. I changed my departure date from Tuesday the 12th to Saturday the 16th of that same week.

I tried this out because statistically speaking; most people fly out on Fridays or Saturdays because it is the start of their weekend. Vacationers most often take a full week of work off. If possible, they will sneak out and take a flight on Friday or Saturday to take advantage of as much of that weekend as possible. Vacation travel sometimes extends past a week long, but most Americans take vacations in full week blocks, and they end up flying on Fridays, Saturdays, and Sundays. It becomes a simple equation at that point. More demand equals higher prices.

As you can see highlighted in dark blue, Saturday is $343 compared to Tuesdays $193. That is $150 dollars difference per ticket! I don't know about you, but that is what I consider to be a sizeable savings.

It is probably pretty safe to say that hardly anyone wants to fly on a Tuesday or Wednesday because of jobs or the kids being in school, but the airlines still have to fill those midweek seats, so they make them cheap.

As you can plainly see from the examples that I have provided, this isn't something that I am just making up. The numbers do not lie in this case so if you can somehow manage to take advantage of the system that is set in place, you could enjoy a decent savings.

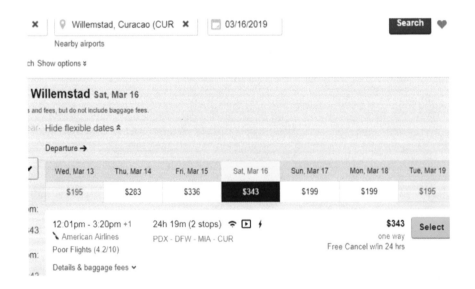

One huge factor in how much your ticket costs is how far ahead of time you book. I read an article by CheapAir that found that a single flight's lowest fare changes an average of 71 times, going up and down by an average of $33 about every four and a half days. That study also found that the best time to book a flight is between three weeks and three and a half months in advance of travel, since fares tend to be within 5 percent of their lowest. Book a little further in advance for spring and summer travel, when demand is high. There was an Expedia/ARC study that found something similar: for most routes, the lowest prices are found 30 days or more ahead of the departure date, and rise sharply after that. All of the studies found that there's no benefit to waiting until the last minute; by and large, you'll end up paying hundreds more than you need to if you go that route.

In direct response to these studies, I conducted my own experiment. I checked my flight to Curacao multiple times during every week and weekend. If you take a moment and refer back to the picture that I posted of my flight information to Willemstad, you will see that my flight on Tuesday March 12th was $193.00. And I booked the flight back on January 8th which was more than two months prior to my departure date. Each and every time I checked, my flight stayed at $193.00. I will ensure that I document some of the changes as they occur.

Now I did see the prices change on the Thursday, Friday and Saturday slots quite a bit. As I checked the prices on February 18th, the price on Thursday had jumped from $283.00 to $338.00. That is a $55.00 jump per person and we were still more than 4 weeks out. Friday went from $287.00 to $342.00, also a $55.00 jump. Saturday went from $345.00 to $395.00 which was a $50.00 increase.

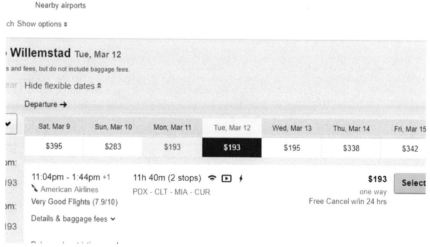

** Screen shot taken Mon Feb 18th, 2019

3

Continuing with the experiment I checked on Expedia.com again on Thursday 2/21/2019 and the price of my flight finally changed. So roughly 19 days out from the flight date and my price finally changed. I guess this falls into the 3 week to 3 and a half month time frame that the CheapAir article I read mentioned. However, the price listed on Tues the 12th didn't change one time in roughly 44 days. In addition, if you look at Monday the 11th, it still didn't change in that amount of time.

Take a look at Tues March 12th which is highlighted in blue. It jumped up to $281.00 compared to $193.00 which is an $88.00 increase. As I mentioned earlier, and oddly enough, Monday the 11th had stayed the same at $193.00.

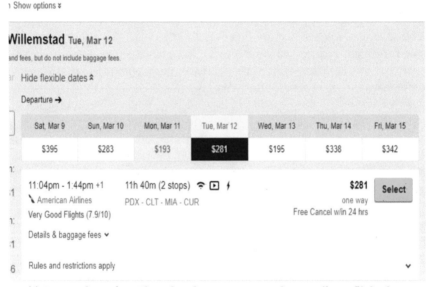

** Screen shot taken Thursday the 21st, 2019. 19 days until our flight date.

I didn't feel like filling the book up with all the changes in pricing as I monitored my flight. But here is a screen shot that I took to show how much it increased at one week and two days away from the departure date.

My flight and every other flight increased significantly at this point. You can see highlighted in blue that my flight has now increased to $406.00 which is a huge $213.00 jump over the $193.00 I paid originally.

As my flight came closer I checked and the prices did change almost every day the closer the flight date came. On Sunday March 10th I checked at 9:15am (I leave on the 12th) and the flight was at $630.00 on Expedia. Once again that is a huge jump from the $193.00 that I paid.

An interesting thing I observed was, now Tuesday is the most expensive day. All of the other days were at around $400 - $500. I have no reasoning or logic to offer as to why Tuesday has jumped up so high, but it did.

So I hope that all of you that are reading this are getting the point that I am trying to drive home. Plan ahead and purchase your tickets quite a ways out from your actual flight date. It will absolutely save you money. The proof is right there in black and white for you to see.

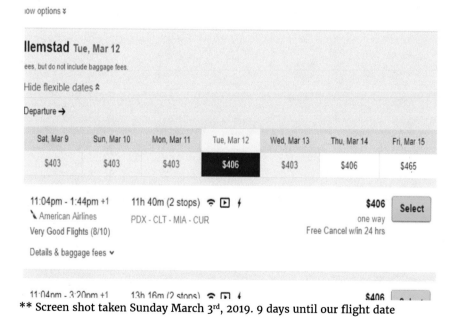

** Screen shot taken Sunday March 3rd, 2019. 9 days until our flight date

Now here is something that you may or may not know about some airlines. You can certainly get a bit of a better deal if you don't care about where you sit. And it just so happens that with American Airlines, the $193 was certainly a good deal and a good viable option, but at that price I would not get a seat choice.

As I mentioned, if sitting next to a companion is important to you, you would have to upgrade from the basic economy fare which did not allow for a seat choice, to the main cabin option which did. If this is a choice you would make, then the price would go from $385.40 to $415.40 which is $15 a piece for you and your companion. (See the illustration/screen shot on the following page).

Now, in reference to main cabin fares that I mentioned; Customers may select a free seat, or pay for a preferred or main cabin extra seat. If a free seat is not available, a seat will either be automatically provided at check-in or at the airport.

Travelers should note that while seat assignments are indeed complimentary for American Airlines passengers in select fare classes, those flying basic economy must pay extra to select their seats in advance (or they will be assigned a seat when they check in).

Once again, if you want the lowest price then you will be choosing the Basic Economy fare. There are some restrictions but you'll still get a comfortable seat in the Main Cabin and enjoy free snacks, soft drinks and inflight entertainment.

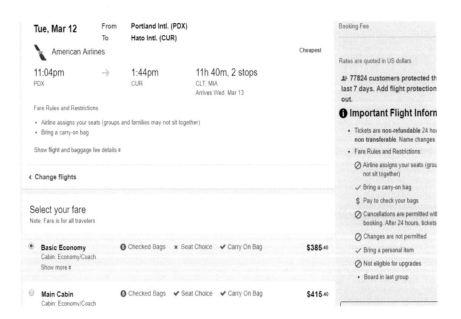

Credit Cards / Miles Cards

Who among you does not know anything about credit cards that earn points or miles?

I am amazed at how many people I talk with that actually do not. As I talk with them I find myself wondering, "Have you been locked away in a closet or something?" How could anyone not know about the benefits of credit cards that earn miles?

This section is for those that may not know much about them. And for those of you reading this that are veteran miles card users, feel free to skip forward. Or, read on through and see if you might pick up some useful information that you didn't know.

For those of us that love to travel, these cards can be a great tool to have in our tool belt. Last year I paid for my flight to Italy and back with my points that I acquired on my card. So if you think of that value alone, that is pretty much worth learning about in my opinion.

Take a look in your wallet. Are your credit cards working for you? If not, then why not? As you think about how many cards you have and how much you use them, doesn't it just make sense to have a card that rewards you in some way for using it?

For me, I try to use my card for everything that I possibly can. I figure if I am spending the money anyway, why not just use my miles credit card to pay for it? I use the Capital One Venture One card and it earns me an unlimited 1.25 miles for every dollar that I spend. In addition, I earned 20,000 bonus miles once I spent $1,000 on purchases within the first 3 months of opening the account. I pay no annual fee to have the card and I received 0% intro APR for 12 months.

Capital one has many other cards available and there are many other companies like Capital One that offers rewards cards. Remember, a little time and some research goes a long way. So take some time and read through as many options as you can to see which card might be the best fit for you. Knowing exactly what card you will pick and why can keep you from making some common and costly mistakes.

It seems basic, but one of the biggest mistakes you can possibly make with a travel rewards card is not earning the welcome bonus. Many of us are wowed by bonuses worth tens or even hundreds of thousands of points, but that only justifies signing up for a card when you actually earn them. There are a couple reasons that I can think of that might make you miss the mark.

The first is that welcome bonuses typically require you to spend a certain amount of money on your card within a certain time frame, like $1,000 within three months, or $5,000 within six months. If you apply for a card (or several cards at once) and the minimum-spending threshold is too high for you to hit (responsibly!), you risk not earning the bonus. That said, a welcome bonus is not worth being reckless with your credit and finances, so do yourself a favor and be sure that you can safely achieve the spending requirement before applying.

As I mentioned above, applying for too many cards in a short period of time can mean you miss hitting the minimum spending requirements for welcome bonuses. In the case of Chase, however, it can also exclude you from being eligible for some of the issuer's best credit cards.

That's because of Chase's so-called 5/24 rule. Put simply, Chase will automatically deny new applications for certain credit cards in its stable if you have opened more than five new credit card accounts, with any issuer, in the preceding 24-month period. While not every Chase card is subject to this rule, major players like the Chase Sapphire Reserve, Ink Business Preferred Credit Card, Southwest Rapid Rewards Premier Credit Card and United Explorer Card are.

If you need to check how many accounts you've opened recently, you can create a free account with Experian or Credit Karma and track the age of your various accounts.

The second is miscalculating the timing in which you must hit that spending requirement. With a welcome bonus, the spending clock starts when you are approved for the card, not when you receive your card. So you could find yourself with several fewer days, or even weeks, to get all those purchases in. If in doubt, call your card issuer and ask what the deadline is.

Another needless and costly mistake is carrying a balance on any card that you might choose. Unless you are enjoying a 0% interest rate, the most intelligent and cost effective choice you can make is to pay off your balance every month. Because even the most valuable points — ones that you can transfer to hotels or airlines for otherwise high-priced rewards — are not likely to be worth anywhere near the interest rate you'll be paying on balances that you carry. And that's to say nothing of the impact carrying a big balance will have on your credit score. So before you use a points-earning card with a high interest rate to make big purchases that you might not be able to pay off quickly, consider instead using a card with a low (or no) APR instead.

Another key point to scrutinize over is a rewards cards annual fee. Travel rewards credit card annual fees range from $0, like mine or on the new Wells Fargo Propel American Express® Card and the Chase Freedom Unlimited, to several hundred, or even several thousand dollars, like on the Amex Centurion (Black) Card.

Many of the top cards have annual fees that hover around the $95 mark, such as the Chase Sapphire Preferred, Capital One Venture Rewards Credit Card, United Explorer Card, Marriott Rewards Premier Plus Credit Card, among many others. Utilizing perks like free checked bags, automatic hotel elite credit or a free anniversary night makes it easy to compensate for a $95 annual fee...if you use them.

Likewise, there are some fantastic premium travel rewards cards charging higher annual fees that can be well worth it. But, only if you maximize their benefits. For instance, cards that charge $450 a year, like the Chase Sapphire Reserve, the Citi Prestige and the Ritz-Carlton Rewards Credit Card, or $550 like The Platinum Card® from American Express, all offer a range of value-added benefits that can help offset their annual fees. All four offer Global Entry or TSA PreCheck application fee reimbursements worth up to $100. All four also offer annual travel credits for various purchases worth between $200-$300 per year and get cardholders into a variety of Priority Pass lounges. But if you're not actually using these benefits, it's not worth paying that high annual fee.

The same is true of airline credit cards that offer lounge access with their specific airline, like the Delta Reserve from American Express, the Citi / AAdvantage Executive World Elite Mastercard and the United MileagePlus Club Card. Each charges a $450 annual fee and will get you into Delta Sky Clubs, American Admirals Clubs and United Clubs, respectively. That's a discount over purchasing outright club membership, but still not worth much if you're not actually using those clubs.

Many issuers have caught on to the fact that people who want travel rewards credit cards actually, you know, travel. That includes internationally. While issuers once charged 2-3% transaction fees on purchases made abroad, many credit cards now waive these fees. Not all, though. Notable exceptions include the Chase Freedom Unlimited (3%) and the Citi ThankYou Preferred Card (3%). Before you go abroad, or even make a purchase from a foreign company while still in the US, read your card's benefits and terms to see whether you might be dinged with extra fees.

Rewards credit cards can be powerful tools to help you maximize your travel strategy, but only if you can leverage benefits like category, transfer and spending bonuses, fee waivers, lounge access and more. Be sure you are getting enough value from your travel credit cards to justify their annual fees, and that you know the terms and conditions of each so you are not hit with fees and other penalties that might erase the value of any points you earn. By doing so, you can reach your travel goals faster and get that much more value from your credit cards.

Frequent Flyer Programs

Airline miles, also known as frequent flyer miles or travel points, are part of a loyalty program offered by airlines and/or credit cards. Typically, you accumulate a set amount of miles based on how far you fly or how much you spend on your credit card. You can then use these miles to buy tickets.

That's simple enough on the surface, but airline miles aren't that cut and dry. First off, the term "miles" doesn't equate to the actual number of miles you can fly—it equates to the number of miles you've flown. Just because you get 2,734 miles for traveling from Seattle to Miami, for example, doesn't mean you get another free flight. The miles you accumulate are more like points in a rewards program. For example, with Frontier's reward program, you get a free roundtrip domestic ticket for every 20,000 miles you acquire. That means it'll take about four roundtrip flights between Miami and Seattle to get enough miles for one free flight.

In the airline miles world, you can get points two ways: by signing up for a service through the airline itself or by signing up for a credit card that offers reward miles. Some credit cards work on any airline, others are for specific airlines. Both have advantages and disadvantages. Either way, the good news is that you can use both at the same time.

Every airline has their own frequent flyer program usually billed as a loyalty program. These are free, and you can accumulate miles by flying with specific airlines. You can sign up for a frequent flyer account with three different airline alliances and you'll earn frequent flyer miles for most flights. Here are links to sign up with the big three:

American Airlines (AA Advantage)

Delta Airlines (SkyMiles)

United Airlines (MileagePlus)

When you sign up for an account, you'll get an account number that you can use for future flight purchases. These services are very straightforward: you earn miles for each flight you take, and when you accumulate enough, you can redeem those miles for a free flight on that airline. Typically speaking, these miles don't expire as long as you're using your account.

When you first sign up you can also redeem miles for old flights. Typically, the grace period for this is anywhere between three months and a year. It's a pain to go through all your old tickets, but it's worth it for the points you'll get and it's a good way to get started. If you need help keeping track of all those points, AwardWallet is a pretty easy way to do so.

Credit card rewards with airline miles work a little differently. Most credit cards rewards give you a certain amount of points per dollar spent. You can then redeem these points for frequent flyer miles, but how much they're worth depends on the credit card. As with any credit card, you'll often have to deal with annual fees, and you only accrue airline points when you pay your card off. Since you probably use your credit card a lot more than you buy airlines tickets, it's usually easier to accrue points through a credit card then it is with just an airline rewards program.

Basically, airline miles are like any other rewards program. You get points for buying stuff, and eventually those points accumulate and you get something for free.

If you don't fly often or fail to stick with the same airline with each trip, it may seem difficult to accumulate enough frequent flyer miles to experience the benefits.

On top of that, some airlines, like Alaska Airlines and United Airlines, have expiration dates for your miles if your account is inactive over a certain period, according to NerdWallet.

You may not think it's worth your while to register as a frequent flyer, but you could be wrong: Some airline loyalty programs offer benefits beyond miles and points for future travel.

Here are some additional benefits of frequent flyer programs that go beyond earning a free or discounted flight.

The simplest and most basic benefit of signing up for a frequent flyer program is that it allows the airline to store all of your information.

When you book a flight with most airlines, you'll only need your login information. You don't have to scramble to find your known traveler number if you have TSA PreCheck or your passport number if you're flying overseas.

The few extra minutes you spend to join a loyalty program will save you time whenever you go to book a flight. Plus, it sets you up to earn points for other benefits.

Airlines vary in the ways they allow passengers to use their miles to pay for extras.

Aside from a seat, Southwest Rapid Rewards won't let you redeem your points for flight amenities like extra bags, security fees, or in-flight drinks. But other airlines have different policies.

Norwegian Rewards allows you to redeem CashPoints for flight-related charges such as baggage and seat reservation fees. And airlines like Delta and American will let you use earned miles for an upgrade to first or business class.

Check with the airlines you like to fly and see what your points can buy you. You might not have enough to cover a flight to Rome, but you could take a suitcase big enough to hold your museum outfits plus your clubwear at no extra charge.

Some airlines allow you to exchange earned miles for vacations, festivals, sporting events, and more.

Tickets to a professional NFL football game, a seven-day cruise to Costa Rica, a Nascar race in Texas, or a chance to visit the Voodoo Music and Arts Experience in

New Orleans are just a few of the packages you can buy or bid for right now through Delta SkyMiles Experiences.

United's MileagePlus program also offers tickets to concerts and a chance to bid on vacation and event packages. If you use your MileagePlus miles to buy tickets to Broadway shows and you're a member of Broadway loyalty program Audience Rewards, you could earn more United miles with each ticket you buy.

Some of these experiences might cost you enough miles that you could have used the points to book a free flight instead. But several free flights might pale in comparison to a dinner and three-night vacation at the exclusive French Laundry resort in Napa Valley, California, which is set at a current bid of 147,000 miles on Delta's auction site.

American Airlines' MagsforMiles program offers a year's subscription to magazines like Travel + Leisure or Real Simple for just 800 miles each, while 1,100 AA miles can get you a year's subscription to Fortune. You can also use AA miles to subscribe to your local newspaper.

You'll need 17,800 miles to get an Alexa smart speaker with your United miles, but you can get a set of wine glasses for just 5,500 miles.

When you get a notice that your miles are about to expire but don't have the time for a quick getaway, check out your airline's website to explore all of its redemption options.

Booking Sites

When you book a hotel room online, you have two different options. You can either book directly with the hotel or through a third party travel site. As a financially-savvy traveler, you are probably wondering if it's cheaper to book hotels directly or on a third party site? Honestly, there is no set cookie cutter answer. The answer depends on your travel plans.

Some occasions that I have found where it is best to book Hotels directly are...

- Booking an award night with points
- Reserve an upgraded room
- Purchase on-site amenity packages

It should goes without saying, but, you can't pay with points on third party sites unless it's a credit card portal like the Chase Ultimate Rewards portal, or if you get a statement credit for travel purchases from your credit card. Rewards nights need to be booked directly with the hotel.

Even if you pay for your room with cash on a third party site, some hotel programs might not credit your account with rewards points unless you book directly. Unlike airline frequent flier programs that will give you points on every flight, hotel policies are more stringent.

Even if you find a better deal or pay the same price on a third party site, not earning points can end up costing you money down the road. To earn loyalty points, you will want to book directly with the hotel.

Hotels generally offer member-only rates that are a few dollars cheaper than the normal rate nightly rate. IHG Rewards Club, for instance, offers an exclusive member discount that is a few dollars cheaper than the non-member rate and can also be cheaper than the third party rate. The member's only rate at the Holiday Inn Express Orlando at SeaWorld is $106.82 per night. The same room costs $109 for non-IHG members if booked directly and also on Priceline and Hotels.com.

Sometimes, hotels keep the luxury rooms and amenity packages to themselves. It can be cheaper to book hotels when you need to buy a breakfast package, parking, or even ticket bundles to local attractions. Third party sites might offer these packages as well, however, the price can be different.

While most third party booking sites have moved away from charging a booking fee. Some still do and this can negate any savings. If you find a cheaper rate on a third party site, always compare a price quote between the hotel and third party site after taxes and fees have been included.

Several third party sites including Expedia and Hotels.com have their own rewards system that can give you the opportunity to earn free hotel nights. I use Hotels.com because they have partnered with Capital one and I get ten times the miles.

There are a few instances it's cheaper to book hotels using a third party site:
- Last minute bookings
- Mystery Deals
- Travel packages
- Non-cancelable reservations
- Local hotels
- Hotwire and Priceline Express Deals

One time it can be cheaper to book a hotel with a third party site is when you book a Hotwire or Priceline Express Deal. The only downside is that you don't know the name of the hotel until after you have paid.

Priceline claims you can save up to 60% with their Express Deals. Hotwire Hot Rates can also save you up to 60% if you wait until the last minute to book. As it's easier for hotels to lower the price on unfilled rooms through third party mystery deals, scour these offers when you want to book on the same day or within the next few days.

Priceline hotel bidding can save you serious money. PRICELINE Mystery deals can save you money by booking in advance, but, you will save the most money by snapping up a same day deal. Booking a "today only" special can be worth the savings, even if you don't collect the hotel loyalty points.

Keep in mind that mystery deals cannot be canceled.

Local and independent hotels can be cheaper than national brands and just as hospitable. With a chain hotel, you can expect the same experience each time and you can also pay more for the uniformity.

To attract visitors that might be wary of staying in "unfamiliar surroundings," local hotels can offer slightly better rates than their competitors.

While you might not earn loyalty points from independent hotels, you can still get free nights when you book through Expedia or Hotels.com that offer free hotel nights after a predetermined amount of stays.

Hotels also offer travel packages that can bundle flights, hotel nights, and rental cars to save you money. You might have an advantage with third party travel packages because some hotels only partner with specific airlines.

Third party travel sites make it possible to bundle any flight with any hotel. If you like this flexibility and understand that packages are usually non-refundable, the savings can be well worth it.

Since package deals are usually non-refundable, you should still price each travel expense separately and also compare the package hotel rate to cancelable nightly rates from the third-party site and the hotel website.

Every big hotel brand also has properties overseas, but that doesn't mean they are always the best deals. Finding overseas sleeping accommodations since chain hotels might only have locations in the largest cities. Staying at a local hotel might be a better option if you know where to look.

The same third-party booking sites you use to browse domestic hotel listings can be used to book international hotel nights. You might also consider using Agoda if you plan on traveling to Asia where you can search hostels, local brands, and international brands all in one place.

As some international destinations might not be as "commercialized" as the U.S. hotel industry is, you might decide to use third party sites just for international travel.

There are no hard-fast rules for when it's cheaper to book hotels directly or when to use a third party site. Hotels like to reward members for their loyalty. Third party sites can be better when you want to scoop up last minute specials or are do not have a preference for a particular brand. Keeping these tips in mind will help you compare hotel prices for your next stay.

Choosing a Vacation Base Camp

Curacao

I would be visiting three islands on this trip. For my particular situation that meant finding and securing a base camp on each island. I would be flying into Curacao first and would be arriving on Wednesday March 13th.

As I mentioned previously, I used Hotels.com because they partnered with Capital One and I could earn ten times the miles if I went through that third party booking site. And as it turned out, I also landed a pretty good deal.

Once on the Hotels.com website, I surfed around the site and looked at different rooms that I thought would work for me. I didn't necessarily have a tight budget to speak of, but I knew that I didn't want to pay more than $200.00 per night for a room.

There were plenty of options and a wide range of rooms to choose from. I could have easily stayed at a cheap place and paid around $70.00 a night. The Curacao Suites Hotel and the Otrobanda Hotel and Casino were around $77.00 per night. Both hotels were only .7 miles to the city center and around 3 miles to Mambo beach. And after reading the 350 plus reviews and seeing a 4.5 rating out of 5 on Trip Advisor, The Curacao Suites Hotel didn't look half bad.

In my mind, cheaper is not necessarily better. As an individual, I don't require much concerning accommodations. Give me some A/C and a comfy bed and I am good. And in some instances that is just fine and I will go that route if I am really concerned about my budget. But in this case I wanted something close to the beach, and a few notches above a basic economy room. Not necessarily lap of luxury, but nice. As I mentioned before, I didn't set a tight budget, but I thought something around the $200.00 (U.S) range should get me something decent. With this in mind, I chose the Papagayo Beach Hotel.

Papagayo Beach Hotel
Jan Thiel Z/N, Jan Thiel, CW
Phone: +59997474333
www.papagayo.com

In addition to being close to the beach, I wanted a hotel that offered an airport shuttle service and a place that was fairly close to the dolphin academy. The airport shuttle was a bit pricey at $50.90 each way, but I felt like it was worth it since I had absolutely no clue where I was going or how to get there. And the hotel arranged everything so it was hassle free.

This hotel had 451 reviews and rated 4.0 out of 5 on Trip Advisor. It ranked #12 of 37 hotels in Curacao. One of the downsides (if you chose to see it that way) was that it was 4.4 miles to Willemstad and 1.6 miles to Mambo beach.

After comparing my price on Hotels.com and the Papagayo.com website, I knew I was getting a pretty good deal so I decided to book it right away. See the example on the next page...

The Papagayo Beach Hotel also has a nice little market called the Van den Tweel Market, right next door which is very convenient. In addition, there is also a Sports and health club called The Challenge, for all of those that intend on keeping up on their work outs while on vacation.

The Hotels beach area is amazing with plenty of places to eat and to find cocktails. And at night, the place is buzzing with activity for those that want to enjoy a little live music.

There are also two separate places to rent cars very close to the Hotel. I decided to rent a car at Jan Thiel Car Rental once I figured out how expensive taxis were. The other spot was a Hertz rent a car. The people at Jan Thiel were very nice, but the downside was that I had to rent the car for a minimum of three days. And at $165.00, I look back and think I should have rented a car at the airport because that would have been more cost effective. However, I'm not totally certain I would have been able to find my hotel since my phone had no service and therefore no GPS.

Papagayo Beach Hotel

Jan Thiel Z/N
Jan Thiel
CW
+59997474333

Hotels.com confirmation number	154792752443
Check-in	Wednesday, March 13, 2019
Check-out	Friday, March 15, 2019 (Before noon local time)
Your stay	2 nights, 1 room
Cancellation policy	Non-refundable
Amount paid	$374.28

Booking on Hotels.com not only got me ten times the points, but I booked an ocean view room for $374.28 (U.S) for two nights. That is $187.14 (U.S) per night if you do the quick math. As an added benefit, I earned and collected 2 nights towards my 10 nights. Once a person reaches 10 nights of stays that are booked through Hotels.com, they earn a free night.

As you can see in the additional example that I have provided on the next page, the ocean view room advertised on Papagayo.com was $206.00 (U.S) per night which did not include the $22.14 of tax recovery charges and service fees. Total that up and it was at $228.14 per night which is $41.00 more per night than on Hotels.com. When I searched on Expedia, the price advertised was $160.00 (U.S) plus the $22.14 for a total of $182.14 (U.S) per night. Just a small amount less than what I paid on Hotels.com.

This Hotel is roughly 400 meters away from the Scooterhut Curacao where you can rent scooters to tour around the island. If you prefer to pedal and get your exercise, the only place I could find that rents bikes and doesn't just have bike tours is Dasia Cycling Curacao. They are located roughly 6 miles from the Hotel in the Rooi Catochi area.

During my stay on this island I had a number of restaurants on my list that I might possibly check out. They all ranked well online and were reasonably close to the Hotel.

- Koko's: TripAdvisor Rating = #6 of 360 Places to eat in Curacao / Cuisines = Dutch, Bar, Street Food / Meals = Breakfast, Lunch, Brunch
- Chill Beach Bar and Grill: TripAdvisor Rating = #27 of 266 Restaurants in Willemstad / Cuisines = Caribbean, Bar, Barbecue / Meals = Lunch, Dinner
- Tinto Restaurant: TripAdvisor Rating = #52 of 291 Places to Eat in Willemstad / Cuisines = Seafood, Grill, Argentinean, International / Meals = Dinner, Drinks
- Zest Mediterranean: Trip Advisor Rating = #77 of 291 Places to Eat in Willemstad / Cuisines = Seafood, Mediterranean, European / Meals = Lunch, Dinner, Brunch, Late Night, Drinks

Curacao has a multitude of hotels available and a wide range of pricing to choose from. A few of the other highly rated hotels for under $200.00 (U.S) were...

La Maya Beach – Spanish Water Luxury Apartments at around $200.00 (U.S)

La Maya Beach Luxury Apartments is a serene property featuring 34 luxury two-bedroom apartments, all with views of a harbor known as the Spanish Water. The modern, upscale apartments have beautiful kitchens and decks facing out onto a lovely pool. However despite the hotel's name, the beach area is underwhelming and the murky water is not great for swimming. There is no restaurant, fitness room, or other amenities on the property. Guests should rent a car in order to access lots of dining and nicer beaches close by, as nothing is within walking distance.

Floris Suite Hotel - Spa & Beach Club at around $186.00 (U.S)

Ranked #18 of 33 Hotels in Willemstad, The Floris Suite Hotel is a sleek, modern adult-only resort that caters to couples and friends who are looking for chic relaxation. This 72-room, upscale hotel makes a statement with its crisp, all-white decor. The excellent pool area is a definite highlight, while there are two nice beaches close by, but not directly connected to the property.

Kura Hulanda Village & Spa at around $160.00 (U.S)

Ranked #18 of 37 hotels in Curacao, This 82-room upscale resort is more than hotel – it is an entire restored 18th-century village, complete with cobblestone alleyways and courtyards peppered with sculptures. The beautiful European and colonial architecture allows guests to feel like they've stepped back in time. It's conveniently located in downtown Willemstad, an area with lots of dining and shopping that also happens to be a UNESCO World Heritage Site. The hotel offers two lovely pools, two restaurants, a spa and an excellent museum.

Bonaire

Friday evening March 15th around 7:45pm I would be taking a quick hop over to the Island of Bonaire. The air travel distance between these two islands is roughly 51 miles and the flight takes around 30 minutes at a cost of $94.00 (U.S) per person.

Bonaire is well known the world over as a diver's paradise so the main purpose for my visit to the island was to enjoy some scuba diving. The island offers scuba diving 24/7, 365 days a year and in a pristine underwater environment with access to many locations for shore and boat diving, it is an award winning diving destination that accommodates every skill level, from beginner to advanced diver. There are 63 official dive sites on Bonaire and 26 more on Klein Bonaire, of which 54 are shore dive sites. The island has more than 350 fish species and 57 species of soft and stony coral. So it stands to reason that this place attracts many divers from all over the world and this is one of the main activities to enjoy when you visit.

As you can imagine, I wanted to find a dive friendly place to stay. My main dive was going to be at the Bari reef so I wanted to stay at a hotel that wasn't too far from that dive site.

There are many great hotels to choose from but I decided on Captain Don's Habitat. Ranked #4 Best Value of 11 Bonaire Resorts, This hotel was only 650 meters from a nice dive site which was something like an eight to 10 minute walk. As was the case for me on Curacao, I also wanted a place that offered an airport shuttle service.

Captain Don's Habitat Dive Operation is a PADI Resort and a SDI 5 Star Professional Development Center. It is centrally located within the resort complex for easy access from all rooms.

Captain Don's Habitat
Kaya Gobernador N. Debrot 103, Kralendijk, BQ
Phone: +5997178290
book@habitatbonaire.com

To check for pricing directly from the hotels website was a little cumbersome. You actually have to fill out a form to have a quote e-mailed to you. In my opinion, this was a little archaic and slow, so I shopped around on other sites to see what pricing I could find.

I enjoy using Expedia because I find it to be fairly easy to use and I often find good pricing on hotels, flights, etc. In addition, as a perk, I also earn points with them. I found that there was availability for the dates that I needed at $146.00 (U.S) per night.

I had already used Hotels.com for my stay on Curacao, so I also checked on that site to see what I could find. My search showed a cost of $150.00 (U.S) per night which was just slightly more than on Expedia. Since I was already making progress towards my 10 nights, I decided that the extra $4.00 a night was no big deal and went with Hotels.com. Besides, in addition to working towards my free night, I was also getting ten times the miles because of the partnership with Capital One that I showed in a previous illustration.

The hotel is less than a mile to Bike Rentals Bonaire where you can rent a bicycle to cruise around the island on. If you prefer a scooter, Scooters Bonaire is less than a mile and a half away from the hotel. Caribe Car Rental is two and a half miles away if renting a car is more your style.

Bonaire isn't quite as populated and busy as Aruba and Curacao, but that doesn't mean that there aren't some great restaurants on the island. Here is a list of a few different places that we wanted to try that also happened to be fairly close to the hotel...

- Julian's Cafe & Restaurant: TripAdvisor Rating = #8 of 94 Restaurants in Kralendijk / Cuisine = Caribbean, Seafood / Meals = Breakfast, Lunch, Dinner
- Mezza Restaurant: TripAdvisor Rating = #1 of 94 Restaurants in Kralendijk / Cuisine = Middle Eastern / Meals = Dinner
- Restaurant Brass Boer: TripAdvisor Rating = #17 of 94 Restaurants in Kralendijk / Cuisine = Dutch, Seafood, International / Meals = Breakfast, Lunch, Dinner
- Cactus Blue On the Beach: TripAdvisor Rating: #9 of 109 Places to Eat in Kralendijk, Bonaire / Cuisine = American, Caribbean, Seafood, Fast Food / Meals = Lunch, Drinks

A few addition hotels that I came across during my searches that are worth mentioning and were highly rated (under $200.00) were ...

Divi Flamingo Beach Resort and Casino at around $189.00 (U.S)

Ranked #18 of 37 hotels in Curacao, Divi Flamingo Resort and Casino is a 129-room oceanfront hotel catering to divers and families. The hotel's grounds are lush and green and there's a house reef within swimming distance from the resort's pier. Simple rooms have vaulted ceilings and are done in pleasant tropical decor with hardwood furniture and island scenes on the walls. Renovations are ongoing until 2017 -- until then, some of the units remain tired. Many of Divi's rooms are ADA compliant and the hotel's main pool has a ramp for wheelchair accessibility. The hotel caters to families and has kid's activities.

Bellafonte Luxury Oceanfront Hotel at around $189.00 (U.S)

Ranked #4 of 22 hotels in Bonaire, Bellafonte Luxury Oceanfront Hotel has 22 individually-owned apartments in a three-and-a-half-pearl package. Despite the hotel's name, this isn't a luxury property, and decor varies from bright and funky to simple and homey. Air-conditioning, free Wi-Fi, and flat-screen TVs come standard, and while most rooms are spacious and have full kitchens, Studios only include kitchenettes and can be small. Bellafonte has an oceanfront soaking pool and its dock provides easy access to the hotel's house reef, a short swim from shore. Snorkeling equipment is free and the hotel has a concierge, but other features are scarce.

Eden Beach at around $136.00 (U.S)

Ranked #7 Best Value of 11 Bonaire Resorts, Eden Beach is a three-pearl, 71-room oceanfront hotel in Kralendijk, Bonaire's shopping and restaurant hub. The hotel offers discounted dive and drive packages, and its lounge-chair and cabana-filled beach is a short ferry from Klein Bonaire, a beautiful undeveloped tropical island. Rooms are modern, if simple, with IKEA furniture and configurations up to two-bedroom suites with full kitchens, balconies, and ocean views. Spice, Eden Beach's oceanfront eatery, serves up international cuisine and a Euro-centric breakfast buffet, though the pool area needs a bit of TLC and the beach can be crowded. The mosquitos can be pretty bad here as well.

Aruba

Sunday March 17th I would take a couple of different hops to get over to Aruba. I would have to hop back over to Curacao first, and this quick hop would cost $151.00 (U.S) and take about 20 minutes. Then a short time later I would hop on a plane again to hop over to Aruba which cost $115.00 and would take about 25 minutes. The air travel distance from Curacao to Aruba is around 70 miles.

I decided to stay at the Wonders Boutique Hotel during my stay in Aruba. One key item that I wanted with each hotel on each island was airport shuttle service and this place has it available (for a fee of course).

Wonders Boutique Hotel
Emmastraat 63, Oranjestad, AW
Phone: +2975820066
https://wondersaruba.com

I decided to stick with my Hotels.com theme because this would add two more nights onto my total. I would now have six nights out of the ten nights that I needed to earn a free night stay. In addition, I would be earning ten times the miles because of the partnership with Capital One and Hotels.com. Through Hotels.com I secured the room for $160.00 (U.S) per night. I did actually search on Expedia and found the same room for $146.00 (U.S) per night.

If you are keeping score, Expedia had better pricing on all three of the hotels that I booked. Not by a huge amount, but in my case I could have saved around $50.00 (U.S) or so if I would have used them. That could be money that I could have spent towards a dinner, scooter rental or whatever. And when you book with Expedia as a member, you also earn points that can benefit you later once you earn enough. My point in mentioning this is to show that it pays to shop around and weigh out for yourself what you consider to be the best deal.

Sadly, this hotel isn't on the beach. However, it is only around 1.5 miles to Surfside Beach which was in the top 10 beaches on just about every search that I looked at online. In addition, It is only around half a mile or so to the city center and three to four miles to Oranjestad. When looking at the map, it was also very close to a number of different Arubus bus stops along route 2 and 1b. Being so close to public transportation would be helpful and make it easier to get around if you decided that you wanted to brave the public transportation and didn't want to walk.

Scoot Tours Aruba is less than a mile from the Wonders Boutique Hotel. It is located down by the Aruba cruise terminal and ship dock area. Or you could walk up to H&S Rentals which was also less than a mile from the Hotel. At either of these places you can rent scooters to get around the island.

Green Bike Aruba has bicycles that you could rent and it is only 600 – 700 meters walk to their location from the Hotel if you wanted to get a little exercise and peddle around the island.

This Hotel had some of the highest ratings that I found when searching online. It scored an exceptional 9.4 out of 10 and scored a five out of five on Trip Advisor. It had 439 reviews to read through which I consider to be more than enough to verify that this place was a pretty safe bet. It also ranked #3 Best Value of 190 places to stay in Aruba.

I like to have some restaurants lined out when I travel even if I don't actually make it to the places that I research. This hotel was conveniently located close to some highly rated restaurants so I was excited to have the opportunity to check some of them out.

Some of my options within a few mile radius of the hotel were...

- Don Jacinto Restaurant and Parilla: Price Range = $10 - $35 / Cuisines = International, Caribbean, Latin, Colombian, South American / Meals = Lunch, Dinner, Breakfast
- Gostoso Restaurant: Price Range = ? / Cuisines = Caribbean, Seafood, European, Portuguese / Meals = Lunch, Dinner, Late Night

- The West Deck: Price Range = $3 - $13 / Cuisines = American, Caribbean, Bar, Seafood, Bahamian, Grill / Meals = Lunch, Dinner, Late Night, Drinks
- El Gaucho: Price Range = $27 - $49 / Cuisines = Steakhouse, Latin, Argentinean / Meals = Lunch, Dinner, Late Night
- The Dutch Pancake House: Price Range = range $5 - $16 / Cuisines = Dutch, European, International / Meals = Breakfast, Lunch, Dinner, Brunch

A few addition hotels that are worth mentioning that were highly rated (under $200.00) when I searched were ...

Club Arias B&B at around $100.00 (U.S)

Ranked #2 Best Value of 190 places to stay in Aruba. Club Arias Bed & Breakfast is a family-run spot in Aruba's quiet southwestern village of Savaneta. Ten suites (and a tiny budget option, The Nook) are set within spacious and well-landscaped garden grounds with plenty of places to lounge. The entire property has a Mediterranean style, from the clay garden accents, to the large faux boulders and grottos, and down to the impressive hand-painted details covering walls, furniture, and signage. All suites include free cooked-to-order breakfast by Chef Gabriel, who also serves up pizza, pasta, wings, and private dinners. This is an ideal place for families or couples looking for local flavor or even just an escape from heavy tourist areas, but it's not on the beach and you will definitely want to consider securing some sort of transportation.

Golden Villas Aruba at around $164.00 (U.S)

Ranked #6 Best Value of 190 places to stay in Aruba. It can be frustrating to feel like a faceless number -- just one of hundreds of guests at a sprawling, chain hotel. That's likely why some guests choose two-and-a-half-pearl Golden Villas, a five-minute drive from either Eagle or Palm Beach. The hotel has eight stylish apartments, all of which are homey, compact, and include full kitchens. Otherwise, there's not much on offer here aside from a small pool and hot tub, but the small size works to the hotel's advantage. Guests get the undivided attention of the hotel's owners, who offer free beach chairs and rides to the grocery store.

Brickell Bay Beach Club & Spa at around $185.00 (U.S)

#9 Best Value of 190 places to stay in Aruba. Brickell Bay Beach Club & Spa is 97-room mid-range boutique around a five-minute walk to Aruba's Palm Beach, the hubbub of the High Rise zone, and a large concentration of restaurants and shopping. Rooms are spacious and contemporary, but the fixed windows and island condensation can breed a musty smell. All units get mini-fridges, free bottles of water, turndown service, luxe toiletries, and huge, fluffy towels. The boutique packs in features such as a club, pool bar, restaurants, and 24-hour fitness center, and business center. It's an ideal adult-only option for anyone looking to be in this bumping area without shelling out for a high-rise resort.

Money Matters

Although Aruba and the Netherlands Antilles have their own currency, US dollars are accepted on all three islands. For tourists that's probably the best form of payment. It can be brought from their home country, it avoids the hassle of having to change money, and most tourist places such as restaurants and stores will simply default to US dollars. The currency on Bonaire and Curaçao is the NAF (Netherlands Antilles Florin) and the currency of Aruba is AFL (Aruba Florin). NAFs and AFLs are both also called "florin" or "guilders" and one US dollar is about 1.8 guilders or florins. Although NAF and AFL are worth about the same, changing from one to the other is usually not a good bargain. AFLs are typically not accepted in Curaçao or Bonaire, and NAFs are typically not accepted in Aruba.

Credit cards and ATM machines:

Cash may be obtained with MasterCard, Visa and American Express cards at credit card offices, banks, in some casinos and via Western Union. ATM machines are available for cards compatible with the Cirrus or Visa Plus system. It might be an idea to check whether your card will work in Aruba by calling 1-800-4-CIRRUS or 1-800-THE-PLUS.

ATM facilities exist at most banks, but also at all gas stations and popular supermarkets. ATM instructions are normally given in Dutch, English, Spanish and Papiamento and cash is normally dispensed in local currency. Some ATM's will also give out cash in US dollars.

All major credit cards are accepted and there are Credit Card & Traveler's checks representatives available (American Express/VISA/MasterCard/Discover) who will help you should you have any problems.

Service charge:

Tipping is not obligatory, but is at the discretion of the visitor. However, some restaurant and bars add a service charge to your bill. When included, the service charge on food and beverage is normally around 10 to 15 percent. At one's own discretion an extra amount can be added for good service.

Electricity

If you are anything like me you are wondering which power plugs and sockets are commonly used on Aruba, Bonaire and Curacao? It would be an important thing to know since just about every gadget and piece of technology that travelers bring on a vacation will need to be recharged with electricity at some point.

From what I could gather from my online searches before actually arriving on the islands was that the power plugs and sockets that are commonly used are of type A, B and F. Check out the following pictures...

- Type A: mainly used in North and Central America, China and Japan. This socket only works with plug A. This socket has no alternative plugs.

- Type B: like type A but with an extra prong for grounding. This socket also works with plug A. This socket also works with plug A.

- Power plugs and sockets type F are used on the islands and are considered the standard plug type. Type F: This socket also works with plug C and E.

Electricity on Aruba

On Aruba the power plugs and sockets are of type A, B and F. The standard voltage is 127 V and the standard frequency is 60 Hz.

What voltage and frequency on Aruba?

You can use your electric appliances on Aruba, if the standard voltage in your country is in between 110 - 127 V (as is in the US, Canada and most South American countries). Manufacturers take small deviations (plus or minus 5%) into account. Be careful if you bring appliances from Japan (100 V).

If the standard voltage in your country is in the range of 220 - 240 V (as is in the UK, Europe, Asia, Africa and Australia), you need a voltage converter on Aruba. Some say you can carefully try to use your appliances on Aruba without a converter. Most likely they won't be damaged, but may not function optimally. If you don't want to take any chances, use a converter. You can also consider a combined power plug adapter/voltage converter.

If the frequency on Aruba (60 Hz) differs from the one in your country, it is not advised to use your appliances. But if there is no voltage difference, you could (at your own risk) try to use the appliance for a short time. Be especially careful with moving, rotating and time related appliances like clocks, shavers and electric fan heaters.

To be sure, check the label on the appliance. Some appliances never need a converter. If the label states 'INPUT: 100-240V, 50/60 Hz' the appliance can be used in all countries in the world. This is common for chargers of tablets/laptops, photo cameras, cell phones, toothbrushes, etc.

Electricity on Bonaire

On Bonaire the power plugs and sockets are of type A, B and F. The standard voltage is 127 / 220 V and the standard frequency is 50 Hz.

Voltage converter needed on Bonaire?

Watch out! On Bonaire more than one voltage is being used (127 / 220 V).

It can depend on the region, the city or even the hotel which voltage you will come across. Your appliances work on 120 V. So please check locally if you can use your appliances! You cannot use your appliances if the local voltage exceeds the maximum voltage of your appliances. You need a voltage converter on Bonaire, when living in the United States! You can find voltage converters at Amazon. Because you also need a power plug adapter, you should consider a combined plug adapter/voltage converter.

Also the frequency on Bonaire (50 Hz) differs from the frequency in the United States (60 Hz). You should use a voltage converter which also changes the frequency, but these are hard to find. If your converter cannot change the frequency, be warned! Be especially careful with moving, rotating and time related appliances like clocks, shavers.

To be sure, check the label on the appliance. Some appliances never need a converter. If the label states 'INPUT: 100-240V, 50/60 Hz' the appliance can be used in all countries in the world. This is common for chargers of tablets/laptops, photo cameras, cell phones, toothbrushes, etc.

Electricity on Curaçao

On Curaçao the power plugs and sockets are of type A, B and F. The standard voltage is 127 / 220 V and the standard frequency is 50 Hz.

What voltage and frequency on Curaçao?

Watch out! On Curaçao more than one voltage is being used (127 / 220 V). It can depend on the region, the city or even the hotel which voltage you will come across. You cannot use your appliances if the local voltage exceeds the maximum voltage of your appliances. You will need a voltage converter!

If the local voltage is less than that in your own country, you need a voltage converter as well. Some say you can carefully try to use your appliances on Curaçao without a converter. Most likely they won't be damaged, but may not function optimally. If you don't want to take any chances, use a converter. You can also consider a combined power plug adapter/voltage converter.

If the frequency on Curaçao (50 Hz) differs from the one in your country, it is not advised to use your appliances. But if there is no voltage difference, you could (at your own risk) try to use the appliance for a short time. Be especially careful with moving, rotating and time related appliances like clocks, shavers and electric fan heaters.

To be sure, check the label on the appliance. Some appliances never need a converter. If the label states 'INPUT: 100-240V, 50/60 Hz' the appliance can be used in all countries in the world. This is common for chargers of tablets/laptops, photo cameras, cell phones, toothbrushes, etc.

Transportation Options

Renting a car
Driving is on the right in Curacao, so there won't be many problems for North Americans, Europeans and most South Americans when zipping around the islands.

Aruba
Aruba has a good network of roads allowing access to most places of interest. If you want to explore Aruba in air conditioned comfort you can do a lot of sightseeing by following the main paved roads, with many types of cars to choose from for this purpose. Several Aruba Car Rental companies are present at the airport where you pick up or drop off your vehicle or you can even request pick-up at your hotel.

The airport isn't the only place that you can secure a car rental. There is a multitude of car rental facilities that you can choose from all over Aruba.

The "down town" area is very easy to get around. There are plenty of land marks and visual ques to use to navigate. The main strip is always easy to make your way back to and all the shopping areas are easy to get to as well. I saw quite a few street signs in the downtown area also. However, if you get outside of town, street signs are not plentiful and you have to look to find some of them on sides of houses.

The traffic signs we are used to in the US are not anything like the signs on the islands. Do your research if you intend on driving so you know what they mean and so you will know how to follow them.

Bonaire
Bonaire is fortunate to have a wide choice of well known, reliable car rental agencies. Even though the island is relatively small in size, a car is one option that might help you to maximize your vacation. Since Bonaire is known as the shore diving capital of the Caribbean, the most popular rental vehicle is the double cabin pick-up truck. You are well advised to secure a reservation in advance, especially around holiday periods. Most agencies do have a minimum age requirement of 23-25 years. You will need to have a credit card and a valid driving license. Almost all of the cars are standard shift, so if an automatic is needed, please make your reservations early. Visitors will find the rental vehicles to be late models and in top shape. If you intend to tour the national park, be advised that a jeep type vehicle or pick-up with a high ground clearance is required.

If you decide not to rent your car at the airport, there are a number of car rental facilities scattered about the island.

I landed at the airport in the evening and picked up my diesel truck from Budget then. This truck looked like a local owned it. Scratches all the way around, dents, the rear bumper was all messed up and the tailgate didn't work. The upside was that it ran fine and got incredible fuel mileage. After all the driving around I did, I only had to put $4.50 in it to fill it up before I returned it.

The major challenge to driving around this island is the complete absence of street signs. My cell phone didn't have any kind of service of course so I didn't have GPS and I couldn't call the Hotel. The car rental place didn't have GPS to rent. And getting directions from anyone is absolutely worthless because they have no clue how to give directions. The map they give you is a joke for any kind of details to follow.

So I ended up driving blindly towards a destination I have never been to, on an island that I have never been on and absolutely no familiarity with. And unless you have been here before, this will be your challenge as well. But in the day time, you can at least get your bearings a little easier.

Long story short... by the grace of God I found it! I can't even recount to you how I found it because I honestly and truly have no idea. My only goal was to hug the coast in hopes of running into the hotel since it was a popular dive destination on the coast.

Curacao

You'll find a stretch mall full of car rental agencies at the airport, in a building left from the arrival area. I suggest you place a reservation for your car in advance online. This will save you time and money when you come to pick up your car. Nothing worse than having to stand in line, only to find out that the car you want is no longer available.

Curaçao is the biggest of the three islands, both in population and size so you might think that it would have a ton of car rental facilities. It does have plenty to choose from but they are mostly on the southern half of the island.

I ended up being lucky and having two facilities very close to my room, so I rented from one of them once I arrived. I was going to need a car to get to the Rif Fort area since it was miles away.

Just like Bonaire, the street sign situation is crappy at best. I just knew a general direction and I knew that if I headed towards the coast off the main road that I would run into it. And luckily, there are some terrain features that are fairly easy to identify during the day.

Taxi

Aruba

Taxis are widely available in Aruba and normally handle up to five passengers per taxi. Infants of 2 years old or younger are not considered in the passenger count.

Taxis in Aruba do not have meters since rates are based on destination rather than mileage and are set by the Aruba Department of Public Traffic. All prices are per taxi not per person. (Maximum five passengers allowed).

On Sundays, official holidays and after 11 p.m. additional charges to the regular rates apply. Taxis can also be hired on an hourly basis for US$45.00 per hour.

The taxi I took from the airport to my room (5.0 miles) was $30.00 and from my room back to the airport was $22.00. That is pretty expensive for a short ride. But both drivers were very friendly and the cabs were clean.

Bonaire

Bonaire lacks public transportation, so taxis offer the quickest means of short-distance travel. Taxis have fixed rates, but be aware that fares increase by as much as 25 percent between 7 p.m. and midnight, and by up to 50 percent between midnight and 6 a.m. Taxis also offer half-day island tours, which cost about $25 per person for up to two passengers.

Curacao

Taxis in Curacao are easily recognized by having a license plate that is marked with the letters "TX". Taxis fares are unmetered, and drivers may have fare-sheets available. A 25% surcharge will be added to taxi fares if there are more than four passengers or if it is before 06:00am or past 11:00pm. There can also be small fees for large or an excessive amount of luggage. Many taxi drivers can also act as tour guides and will take passengers to different parts of the island. Fares are per taxi, not per person!!!

Example Taxi Fares / Call a Taxi: +(5999) 869 0747
- From Airport to Jan Thiel area: USD $38 - USD $45
- From Airport to Otrobanda (Marriott, Floris Suite, Hilton): USD $20 - USD $28
- From Airport to Lions Dive & Beach Resort (Mambo Beach): USD $30 - USD $35

Bus

Aruba

Getting around by bus is one of the easiest ways to get where you want on Aruba. Especially the supermarkets and all beaches are easy to reach by bus, and you will not have to walk miles from the bus stop once you're there. For going to a restaurant or sightseeing it is still recommended to either rent a car or take a taxi.

All Buses to Malmok or Arashi stop in front of all Hotels starting with Bushiri Beach Resort. Visible on the Bus is a sign denoting the Hotel area, Hotel or town where the bus will stop.

Schedules: Monday to Saturday

Fare: US$ 2.30 one way.

All Buses to Malmok or Arashi stop in front of all Hotels starting with ex-Bushiri Beach Resort.

The bus does not stop at either Divi Divi, Casa del Mar, Aruba Beach Club, Manchebo, Bucuti & Tara Beach Resorts or Costa Linda - the closest stop is the one near the Hospital. Visible on the Bus is a sign denoting either Hotel area, Hotels or Palm Beach.

Bonaire

There is an informal bus system on the island that utilizes vans, but for the most part there is no formal public bus system in place.

Curacao

The bus company on Curacao is Autobus Bedrijf Curacao. The public transport on Curacao is very limited.

You can even go sightseeing by bus. Curaçao offers two kinds of public transportation: the large busses, which are called 'Konvooi', go for a longer distance, and on most urban routes you will find collective cars (max. 9 p.) or vans called 'bus' (they have BUS on their registration plates).

The major bus terminals are located outside the postal office at the 'Waaigat' in Punda, and next to the underpass in Otrobanda. The large busses cover 12 routes departing from the terminal located in Punda, and 9 routes departing from the terminal in Otrobanda. These routes cover most parts of the island, and can bring you too many attractions such as beaches, shopping areas, and parks.

Most city busses go once every hour and every two hours a bus goes westward, less frequent on Sundays. At the bus station at Otrobanda a schedule (Buki di Bus) is available.

I sat at a bust stop for quite some time and a bus never came by, so I gave up on the idea and just got a cab instead.

Motorcycle/Scooter

Aruba

Due to the island's relatively flat terrain and cool trade winds, these are some of the most popular forms of personal transportation on the island. **Scooters** and mopeds can take you on and off road to explore everything the island has to offer. Harley-Davidson riders will even find that motorcycles are very popular on Aruba, as well.

Because Aruba's Scooters and mopeds are so popular, it is a good idea to make reservations, particularly during the heavily-traveled peak season. If you are considering seeing the sights at a slower pace, you will encounter multiple different places that can help.

If you want to go riding, you might want to contact George's Motorcycles, one of the top scooter rental agencies in Oranjestad. Check out their scooter rentals which are even cheaper than the bigger motorcycles. They are situated in Oranjestad, in western Aruba.

Another good option is Trikes Aruba. All Trikes are driven like a car and there are Automatic Trikes and Manual Trikes. Trikes Aruba provides complete instructions and a test drive at the beginning of the tour. You can call them at (297) 738-7453.

Because Aruba is a busy island, it is generally not recommended that vacationers rent Scooters as a primary mode of transportation. While they are an ideal form of leisure transportation, traffic and street conditions can be very confusing for foreigners. Driving is done on the right side of the street, and it is not unusual to have heavy traffic on the roads during rush hour.

When vacationing on Aruba, scooters are excellent ways to see the island's more remote areas, offering vacationers a great chance to enjoy the fresh air and famous scenery. Reasonable rates make two-wheeling adventures available to almost everyone, and excursions to the Aruban countryside are made more pleasant by the independence allowed by Scooters.

Bonaire

Not everyone who visits the island rents a car. The best thing next to walking is to rent a scooter or one of the quads. A number of shops now offer the chance to feel the breeze blow through your hair while on board one of these "open air" vehicles. The same rules that apply for car rentals also apply to these motorized forms of transport. For the real freedom lovers, Harley Davidson's are lined up awaiting new riders! Remember, a license and credit card will need to be shown.

Curacao

As I mention for the other islands, a scooter is a good cost effective way to get around. Just keep in mind, if you plan on transporting lots of extra items, a scooter may not be your best bet.

Bicycle

Aruba

Aruba's rugged countryside is one of the most ideal playgrounds for mountain/trail biking. Aruba also has self-service, street-side bike rental stations at various points within the hotel areas.

Whether it's a leisurely ride on a street bike or a thrilling, adrenaline-pumping trail ride through the countryside, experiencing Aruba by bike could be a unique addition to your vacation experiences.

Bonaire

Bicycle transportation is not particularly common on Bonaire, but it is possible. There are no bike lanes and the roads are often narrow, but even on the major routes, speeds are fairly slow and motorists tend to give cyclists a wide berth.

For the real adventurers, a number of bike rental shops are on hand to rent everything from sedate touring bikes to rugged mountain models that are sure to challenge anyone interested in navigating the miles of marked bike trails.

Though a car allows for more long-distance travel, renting a bike lets you experience Bonaire's coastal vistas in a more intimate way. You can rent a bike on your own at Cycle Bonaire (one of the island's rental shops), or you can take a guided mountain-bike tour and ride along the paths of Washington Slagbaai National Park. Bonaire Tours & Vacations offers three-hour bike excursions; prices vary depending on your chosen route.

Curacao

For a Dutch island, Curaçao is surprisingly lacking in bike lanes and other cycling facilities. Traffic can be perilous in Willemstad, but once you get out of the city there's some pleasant cycling on country and coastal roads. Bicycles are available for rental at many resorts.

If you can get your hands on a mountain bike, there are some fantastic trails in Christoffel National Park and at Playa Portomari.

Curaçao has beautiful landscaping and scenery, and riding a bike lets you feel the warm tropical breezes across your face while getting around the island.

By renting a bike or moped while vacationing in Curaçao, you have all the independence of touring the island at your pace, without paying the high costs of renting a car. Bikes are a good way to quickly get around town during traffic jams, because you can maneuver around bulkier vehicles. Nature lovers will enjoy the ability to casually tour the island's countryside. Two-wheeled travel allows you to view the island's nature sites, soak up the gorgeous sun, and venture away from the center of the city.

Walking

Aruba

Being on vacation doesn't mean you have to get out of shape! Aruba's beautiful weather and mostly flat terrain, makes walking and hiking a pleasure for everyone. If you're looking to experience Aruba's monuments up close, a walking tour might be the best way to do it. Local Experts make the trip more enjoyable, allowing you to appreciate Aruba's rich history while having fun. You can also take a leisurely hike, and capture moments you would otherwise not experience from inside a tour bus. For the best experience, don't forget to wear comfortable shoes, apply sun protection, and drink plenty of water throughout your walk.

I walked almost 13 miles during my few days there. The place I stayed at was about a mile off the strip and I could see the back side of the Renaissance Hotel as I looked or walked down Emmastraat. The Renaissance Hotel was a great marker to use as a landmark to navigate around.

The main drag and "downtown" area were very easy to find your way around. I didn't really get too far outside of the downtown area, but I don't think you could easily get lost if you were walking around.

Bonaire

Kralendijk is relatively small and can be easily navigated on foot. Those staying outside the center or those wishing to explore the island will want to arrange for car rentals or motorized transportation.

I walked through the main part of Kralendijk and didn't have any problems finding my way around. It is pretty much right on the water, so you are just walking along a boardwalk more or less. There are lots of places to eat and places to shop in this area.

Curacao

Rif Fort was the main area that I walked around. I crossed St. Anna Bay by way of the Queen Emma Bridge over to Punda and walked around there quite a bit as well. All of Willemstad had plenty of places to eat and plenty of places for those of you that like to shop.

I also walked from my Hotel to the Dolphin Academy because the lady behind the desk said that customers did it all the time and that it only took around 15 minutes. The one cautionary note she passed onto me was that I might want to wear shoes because there is a small spot that is a little rough.

Take a look at the picture with the rocks and the yellow paint on the following page.

The "15 minute" hike that I went on was more like 45 minutes because I literally had to rock climb on the rocky cliffs. Luckily someone has spray painted small spots on the rocks to somewhat mark the "path."

As you can imagine since she made it seem so mellow, I didn't wear shoes at all. I just wore my flip flops! What a mistake that was. There were thick thorns in various parts of the trail and I caught a few of them along the way. Luckily, I didn't fall and break my neck.

The end result was that I made it to the Dolphin Academy on time to do my scheduled dive.

Places to eat

Aruba

The Dutch Pancake House

The Dutch Pancake House is a family friendly restaurant that is ideal for breakfast, lunch and dinner with your whole family. This restaurant offers a wide selection of Dutch pancakes, poffertjes, eggs and other delicious menu items such as special dinner pancakes, schnitzels, and desserts. Their authentic Dutch pancakes are all handmade and baked with only the best fresh ingredients available on the island. They proudly received Aruba's first 'Best Breakfast in Aruba' award. It is only about a mile from our hotel.

It is located at the Renaissance Marketplace at ...

Lloyd G. Smith Blvd 9, Oranjestad, Aruba

Tel: +297 - 583 7180

info@thedutchpancakehouse.com

It rated 4.5 out of 5 stars on the online searches that I found with 2,154 reviews. It ranked #15 of 180 Restaurants in Oranjestad on TripAdvisor.

El Gaucho

El Gaucho is a typical Argentine Steakhouse, famous for serving succulent steaks grilled the Argentinian way.

It is located at ...

Wilhelminastraat 80, Oranjestad, Aruba

Tel: +297 - 582 3677

https://www.elgaucho-aruba.com

El Gaucho scored 4.5 out of 5 stars with 3,637 reviews. It ranked #23 of 180 Restaurants in Oranjestad on TripAdvisor. It was also the Certificate of Excellence2015 - 2018 Winner.

Gostoso Restaurant

Gostoso Restaurant is a local favorite that serves a blend of both Portuguese and Aruban Cuisine.

It is located at ...

Caya Ing. Roland H. Lacle 12, Oranjestad, Aruba

Tel: +297 - 588 0053

Gostoso Restaurant scored 4.5 out of 5 stars according to the online searches I came across with 1,299 reviews. It also ranked #5 of 180 Restaurants in Oranjestad on TripAdvisor.

Bonaire

Mezze

Mezze is a contemporary Middle Eastern restaurant that interprets the authentic flavors of the Middle East with a modern approach in Bonaire.

They pride themselves in using only fresh ingredients and providing impeccable, daily prepared items in the spirit of sharing.

The soul of Mezze is the pita bread, baked to order in their wood-fired oven to accompany the creamy and nutty hummus; and the sizzling skewers of meat grilled over hardwood charcoal. Mezze's menu offers small plates and encourages guests to sample the large variety of cultural influences on the Middle Eastern cuisine such as the Eastern Mediterranean.

Enjoy dinner here while relaxing and enjoying their bountiful Middle Eastern selection of food with a carefully selected wine menu. All of this with an impeccable ocean-front view belonging to Bonaire.

Located at...

Kaya Charles E.B Hellmund 17 | Opposite side of the Bonaire's main Pier, Kralendijk, Bonaire

+599 786 8631

http://www.mezzebonaire.com

Mezze scored 4.5 out of 5 stars and had 477 reviews. It ranked #1 of 108 Restaurants in Bonaire and was a TripAdvisor Certificate of Excellence2018 Winner.

Gogreen

Gogreen is dedicated to supporting a balanced and healthy lifestyle of the individual. All Gogreen´s food is prepared fresh on location each day, using intuitive indian cooking principles. Their menu changes daily based on the availability of fresh ingredients and the personal creativity of the chef. They request and prefer that you please make reservations so they can better prepare and serve you with fresh foods.

Located at...

Kaya Gobernador N Debrot 49, Kralendijk 3109, Bonaire

+599 700 5488

http://gogreenayurveda.com

Gogreen scored 5 out of 5 stars and had 130 reviews. It ranked #2 of 108 Restaurants in Bonaire and was a TripAdvisor Certificate of Excellence2016 - 2018 Winner.

Eddy's Bar & Restaurant

They are a family run and owned restaurant, when you are there, you can tell that they want you to feel at home. Their Cuisine is a delicious melting pot, drawing ingredients and methods from French, Colombian and Venezuelan cuisine, combining them with the native foods and recipes of the island. Try this place out and experience these unique flavors and relaxed & friendly ambiance of the Caribbean.

Eddy's Bar & Restaurant scored 4.5 out of 5 stars and had 702 reviews. It ranked #3 of 108 Restaurants in Kralendijk, Bonaire and was a TripAdvisor Certificate of Excellence2015 – 2018 Winner.

Curacao

La Boheme Curacao

La Bohème Curacao is an atypical bistro, run by a Chilean family with a very multicultural staff. You can tell that they strive to serve everyone as if they were part of their family in a very cozy yet informal atmosphere. Being located in one of the most multicultural islands in the Caribbean they celebrate their differences, imprinting them in their menu and decoration styles. They mix flavors from all over South America to create a very unique mosaic. If you want to experience a bohemian meal in the heart of Punda, give this place a try. No matter what language you speak, they might even serve you in your own language!

Located in Punda at ...

Columbusstraat # 4 | Punda, Willemstad, Curacao

+599 9 465 1966

https://www.labohemecuracao.com

La Boheme Curacao scored 4.5 out of 5 stars and had 447 reviews. It ranked #3 of 267 Restaurants in Willemstad and was a TripAdvisor Certificate of Excellence2018 Winner.

The Wine Cellar

The Wine Cellar is a popular and exclusive French restaurant in the Caribbean; the perfect place for a delicious lunch or a romantic dinner. Owned by Nico Cornelisse, a 'Maitre Rotisseur' from Holland , it has been a renowned dining room in Curaçao for more than thirty years.

The kitchen combines authentic French cuisine with Caribbean flair, adding a personal signature. Watching over your health, the chefs always include the freshest herbs and the finest Virgin Olive Oil in their cooking. The menu features dishes like fresh Grouper and lobster, while the finest rack of Lamb from Holland is flown-in weekly. A choice of the world's most popular wines complements the exquisite cuisine. Finish your meal with a warm walnut- and cashew pie, Crepes Suzette or a light quesillo flan. Italian coffee is served with a selection of Dutch chocolates.

Located at ...

Ooststraat at Concordiastraat, Willemstad, Curacao

+599 9 461 2178

http://www.thewinecellarcuracao.com

The Wine Cellar scored 4.5 out of 5 and had 1500 reviews. It ranked #1 of 267 Restaurants in Willemstad and was the TripAdvisor Travelers' Choice2018 Winner.

Mosa

Mosa promotes a shared dining experience for friends and family. They offer International Tapas with an introduction to Bistronomy! In other words, casual fine dining. All dishes are prepared with fresh high quality ingredients and can be paired with an exciting arrangement of wine"!

Located at...

Penstraat # 41 | Pietermaai, Willemstad, Curacao

+599 9 668 0232

http://www.mosarestaurant.com

Mosa scored 4.5 out of 5 stars and had 374 reviews. It ranked #4 of 267 Restaurants in Willemstad and was a TripAdvisor Certificate of Excellence2018 Winner.

Attractions

Aruba

There is pretty much something to do for just about everyone on Aruba.

Aruba's beaches are probably one of the biggest attractions on the island. Even though it's great to spend your day relaxing on the beach, Aruba offers plenty of other attractions and activities that are well worth exploring during your stay.

Days on Aruba are full of scuba diving off Hadicurari Beach, seeing the natural wonders of Arikok National Park or shopping for Dutch cheese in Oranjestad. You can take your tots to the calm waters of Baby Beach and slightly older kids to the Donkey Sanctuary or Ostrich Farm. But save some energy for evening hours, when the flashing lights of a Palm Beach casino or the live music of an Oranjestad pub beckon.

Bonaire

Bonaire's National Marine Park offers a total of 89 dive sites (most of which are shore dives), it is home to over 57 species of soft and stony coral and there are more than 350 recorded fish species.

In addition to being a diver's paradise, Bonaire has a wide range of nature and outdoor activities to keep you busy. There is kite boarding and windsurfing in the majestic, blue ocean, kayaking in the mangroves or calm bay and mountain biking or bird watching on land.

Curacao

- Visit Klein Curacao
- Landhuis Chobolobo: Home of the Genuine Curacao Liqueur
- Deep Sea Fishing
- Golf
- Shopping
- Sailing
- Mountain Biking
- Paddle Boarding
- Windsurfing

Dolphin Academy

Bapor Kibrá, Willemstad, Curaçao
+599 9 465 8900
https://dolphin-academy.com/

Visitors to the Dolphin Academy get a chance to meet dolphins in natural lagoons or the open sea. They afford you an opportunity to achieve authentic dolphin-human interaction, which is also reinforced in a responsible and educational way through their different programs.

Dolphin Encounter -
An experience for all ages! While standing in waist-deep water, you will be able to gently pet a dolphin who will give you a kiss and a handshake!
The Dolphin Encounter is an intimate and interactive experience, which lasts for approximately 20 minutes. The whole experience will be about 1,5 hour.
$99.00

Dolphin Swim -
Enjoy the unique and intimate experience of genuine interaction while swimming with dolphins in the natural lagoon.
Your time in the water is approximately 30 minutes. The whole experience will be about 1,5 hour.
$174.00

Dolphin (snorkel) Free Dive –
Enjoy the intimate and unique experience of genuine interaction while snorkeling with dolphins in the natural lagoon.

Your time in the water is approximately 30 minutes. The whole experience will be about 1,5 hour.

$184.00

Dolphin Scuba Encounter –

Get up close and personal with a dolphin in their world as you scuba in the lagoon.

Reservations for this experience can only be made by contacting Ocean Encounters directly.

Your time underwater is approximately 30 minutes.

$303.00

Gear rental is extra.

Purchase video, approx. 11 minutes in length on thumb drive $70.00

To watch this video you can go to my YouTube channel to view it. Go to YouTube and search under Bryan Kelley, curiouskelley.com or Dolphin Encounter Movie Curacao. You can also go directly to my website at curiouskelley.com and find this video link on the post about the ABC Islands at the bottom of the post.

Best Time to Visit

One of the good things about these islands is that they are close to the equator which means that they have a year-round excellent climate. The islands have an average temperature of 27 degrees Celsius which is around 80 degrees Fahrenheit. Some periods may be slightly drier or wetter. Determining an ideal time for your visit is therefore merely up to you: would you like to experience Carnival or one of the other great festivals? Would you like to escape the cold winters at home? If you can, try traveling in the low season. Generally hotel and ticket prices are higher during the holidays in December and around the big festivals.

May to November is considered the off-peak season. During these months, you'll typically find the lowest airfares and hotel rates, with rooms often priced up to 50 percent lower than they are in the high season (especially during summer). Plus, you won't be vying for beach chairs with multitudes of other vacationers.

If you've come to dive or snorkel, you'll enjoy good visibility throughout the year. Because the islands are located outside the hurricane belt, their marine life is unaffected by seasonal changes.

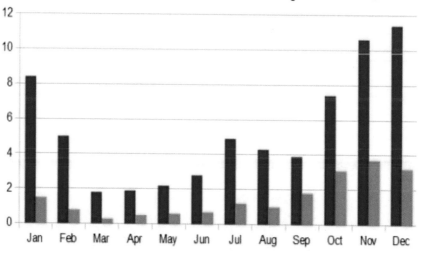

⁞ Monthly Rainfall

■ Rain Days ■ Inches

Hurricanes

The ABC Islands are part of the so-called Leeward Islands, which are geographically located outside the Hurricane Belt. As on other islands strong winds may pass, but rarely pose a threat. Of course, even though these islands are outside the hurricane belt, one can never 100 % predict nature. There are some differences in precipitation throughout the year. March till June are the driest months, with sometimes no rain at all. Some rain may fall during January, July, August and September. October, November and December are the wettest months. Generally speaking showers are short, intense and offer a refreshing break from the sun heat.

Aruba lies on the fringes of the hurricane belt, and locals like to boast that only six hurricanes have passed within 62 miles of this Dutch island over the past 140 years (the last two were Janet in 1955 and Ivan in 2004, while the tail of Matthew whipped the island's beaches in 2016). That means with no direct hits the odds are in your favor that you can head worry free to this welcoming island with its popular Palm Beach and Eagle Beach resort areas, casinos and watersports.

Like Aruba, Bonaire lies on the outer edge of the hurricane belt and has a history of avoiding major storms. Yet, there have been a few close calls: In 2008 Omar got near enough to destroy many of the islands shallow coral reefs and in 2016 Matthew skirted the island and storm surges caused some beach erosion. But if you are a diver, love arid landscapes or want to see pink flamingos, Bonaire is a pretty safe bet for late summer or fall visit.

The "C" of the ABC Islands has not generally been in the path of major hurricanes. That said, in 2010 Tomas weakened to tropical storm status as it approached the Dutch island, stalled and caused heavy flooding. A few years before that, Felix (2007) passed to the north and drenched Curacao and Omar (2008) formed nearby and also dumped heavy rain. But since a direct hit is rare, this island remains a good option if you want to experience the historic ambience of Willemstad and the beauty of its cave lined coasts, secluded beaches and vivid blue water.

Internet Services

Many hotels, bars, restaurants and other locations on the islands provide Wifi services, often for free. In some tourist areas like the city center the government provides a free public Wifi network. Mobile 4g/3g services are available, but roaming charges can be quite high. If you plan or need extensive use of Internet a good solution might be to rent a personal mobile 4g/wifi router (a Mifi) for the length of your stay at one of the local telecom operators.

During my stay just about everywhere I went offered Wifi. It may have not always been powerful enough to upload a photo on Facebook, but at least it was available.

Languages

Papiamento is a Creole language containing elements of Spanish, Portuguese, Dutch, English and French, as well as Arawakan and African languages. It is spoken by about 330,000 people in Curaçao, Bonaire and Aruba, which were formerly known as the Netherlands Antilles. There are also Papiamento speakers in the Netherlands and Saint Maarten. In Curaçao and Bonaire the language is known as Papiamentu, and it is known as Papiamento in Aruba.

Papiamentu, Dutch and English are the official languages of Curaçao; Papiamentu and Dutch are the official languages in Bonaire, and in Aruba the official languages are Papiamento and Dutch.

Spanish, English and Dutch are also widely spoken. Some hotels even offer their service in more languages and you can check with your hotel for details.

Disappointments

Overall, I truly have no complaints. The islands were a great choice and I would go back again in a heartbeat.

I think my biggest disappointment was the lack of road signs on Bonaire and Curacao. If you have a couple of days just to drive around and take in the lay of the land, I guess you would be fine. However, I know that I don't want to waste a bunch of time that I just don't have to drive around and learn.

So not knowing where you are going or how to get there limits you a bit. I would have liked to have explored more restaurants, but I couldn't find them on my own and the directions I received from the locals were absolutely horrendous.

Summary

These three islands with their desert like terrain and lunar like interior landscapes are a vacationers dream. Travelers from all over the world come to soak up the dependable sunshine (it rains less here than anywhere else in the Caribbean), enjoy the spectacular beaches, and try their hand at the many watersports that are available. The wealth of marine life off their shores makes for a divers and snorkelers paradise.

If you're trying to choose just one among the Dutch ABC islands, go to Aruba for beaches and gambling, Bonaire for scuba diving, and Curaçao for little cove beaches, shopping, history, and its distinctive "Dutch in the Caribbean" culture.

But if your anything like me...make sure you make it to all three.

Anyone reading this book that hasn't already purchased it can find it at Amazon.com in print version as well as for a Kindle device.

If you have read this book, please take the time to visit Amazon.com to write your honest review.

As I mentioned throughout the book, you can follow my adventures on my blog at curiouskelley.com. You can watch videos of some of my adventures on my YouTube channels at curiouskelly and Bryan Kelley. If you visit either one, please take a moment and subscribe.

Made in the USA
Columbia, SC
10 December 2020